THE TRIANGLE SHIRTWAIST FACTORY FIRE

A HISTORY PERSPECTIVES BOOK

Rachel A. Bailey

Published in the United States of America
by Cherry Lake Publishing
Ann Arbor, Michigan
www.cherrylakepublishing.com

Consultants: Gerald Markowitz, Distinguished Professor of History, John Jay College and
Graduate Center, City University of New York; Marla Conn, ReadAbility, Inc.
Editorial direction: Red Line Editorial
Book design: Sleeping Bear Press

Photo Credits: Library of Congress, cover (left), cover (middle), cover (right), 1 (left),
1 (middle), 1 (right), 4; Bettmann/Corbis, 6, 12, 30; Public Domain, 8; George Grantham
Bain Collection/Library of Congress, 10, 17, 25; H.W. Sierichs/Library of Congress, 14;
Underwood & Underwood/Corbis, 19, 26; Kirn Vintage Stock/Corbis, 22

Library of Congress Cataloging-in-Publication Data
Bailey, Rachel A.
  The Triangle Shirtwaist Factory fire / Rachel A. Bailey.
      pages cm. -- (Perspectives library)
  Includes bibliographical references and index.
  ISBN 978-1-63137-620-7 (hardcover) -- ISBN 978-1-63137-665-8 (pbk.)
-- ISBN 978-1-63137-710-5 (pdf ebook) -- ISBN 978-1-63137-755-6 (ebook)
1. Triangle Shirtwaist Company--Fire, 1911--Juvenile literature. 2. New York
(N.Y.)--History--1898-1951--Juvenile literature. 3. Clothing factories--New York
(State)--New York--Safety measures--History--20th century--Juvenile literature.
4. Labor laws and legislation--New York (State)--New York--History--20th century
--Juvenile literature. I. Title.
F128.5.B247 2014
974.7'1041--dc23
                              2014004587

Cherry Lake Publishing would like to acknowledge the work of
The Partnership for 21st Century Skills. Please visit *www.p21.org*
for more information.

Printed in the United States of America
Corporate Graphics Inc.
July 2014

TABLE OF CONTENTS

In this book you will read about the Triangle Shirtwaist Factory fire from three perspectives. Each perspective is based on real things that happened to real people who witnessed or experienced the fire. As you'll see, the same event can look different depending on one's point of view.

1

Anna Goldstein
Factory Worker

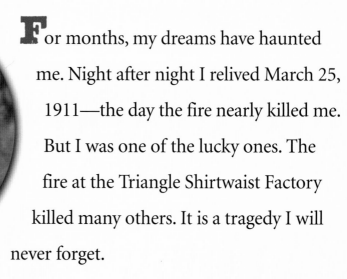

For months, my dreams have haunted me. Night after night I relived March 25, 1911—the day the fire nearly killed me. But I was one of the lucky ones. The fire at the Triangle Shirtwaist Factory killed many others. It is a tragedy I will never forget.

My family and I were strangers in this land—recent Jewish **immigrants** from Russia.

Father came first to the United States. He worked as a shoemaker. It took him a year to save enough money to send for us. In February 1909, we joined him in New York City. We lived in a Jewish **tenement** building in the city's Lower East Side.

It didn't take Father long to realize that he couldn't support us all. Although Mother cleaned a few houses, her income was not enough. Father still felt that she should be at home cooking, cleaning, and taking care of Ester, who was seven, and Aleksander, who was only two. Since I was almost 14, my parents felt that I should work to help pay the bills and rent.

We decided that a job in the garment industry would be fitting for me. Mother taught me how to sew when I was very young. There were many jobs available because

THINK ABOUT IT

▶ Determine the main point of this paragraph. Pick out one piece of evidence to support it.

◄ *The Triangle Shirtwaist Factory was in the Asch Building in New York City.*

of the popular shirtwaist. My older cousin Rosie was a machine operator at the Triangle Shirtwaist Factory. The company was located on the top three floors of the Asch Building near Washington Square Park.

In June, Rosie's **foreman** hired me as a machine operator. I earned around seven dollars a week. This was what I made before I paid for my own needles and thread. The more shirts I sewed, the larger my paycheck was. I had to be careful not to make a mistake when I sewed or my foreman would dock my pay. He also took wages from our paychecks if we were five minutes late or even if we stayed in the bathroom too long. I did not think this was fair.

Rows of sewing machines sat crammed together on long wooden tables. When we sat down to sew, it was difficult for others to walk through the aisles. On the floor were baskets filled with fabric and cloth scraps.

THE POPULAR SHIRTWAIST

The shirtwaist was the height of fashion in the early twentieth century. It was a ready-to-wear button-down woman's blouse. Available in a variety of colors, its simple design was modeled after men's shirts. The shirt became the standard shirt of working women.

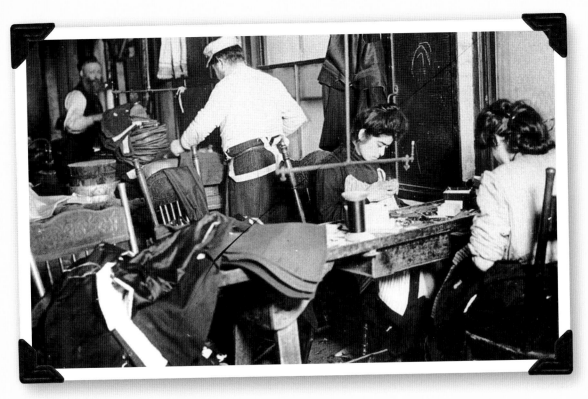

▲ *Garment workers labored in crowded conditions in the early 1900s.*

The 12-hour days dragged by. I wasn't allowed to talk to the other girls. During the winter busy season, we worked close to 14 hours each day. I dreaded going to work every day. But my family needed the small amount of money I made. We called the Triangle a prison. Employees had to work very hard for little pay. Something needed to be done!

On November 22, 1909, Rosie and I attended a meeting. It was organized by the International Ladies Garment Workers' **Union**. The purpose of the union was to improve working conditions for garment workers. At least 1,000 people packed into the hall for the meeting that night.

After hours of debate, a young Jewish girl named Clara Lemlich asked if she could say a few words. In Yiddish, a language spoken by European Jews, she explained how tired she was of all the talking. She felt it was time for everyone to go on a general **strike**. When Clara finished, the crowd roared and clapped wildly. They then voted to strike.

Two mornings later, Rosie and I joined the **picket** line. We also marched downtown with workers from other clothing factories. Within days, many employers caved in to the demands of the union. The owners of the Triangle did not give in.

The owners instead hired people to hurt us. On one cold morning, a group of poorly dressed

▲ *Garment workers joined together to strike for better pay and working conditions in 1910.*

women attacked our picket line. A skinny, greasy-haired woman kicked, punched, and clawed at me. I was a bloody mess! When the police came with their batons to break up the fight, they arrested us strikers. They did not arrest the people who attacked us!

Incidents like this went on for several weeks until the strike ended in February 1910. The Triangle owners gave us our jobs back. We got shorter working hours and a slight pay raise.

Life was bearable until March 25, 1911. The bell sounded at 4:30 p.m. signaling the end of the workday. I scanned the aisles for Rosie. We were going to meet her fiancé for dinner. She had just gotten engaged last week. Her gold ring was gorgeous!

With no sign of Rosie, I went to the dressing room to get my coat and scarf. When I came out, I heard someone scream, "Fire!" Outside the dressing room, smoke poured into the back staircase and freight elevator. Flames twisted in from the windows. Girls with their hair ablaze jumped up on the sewing

SECOND SOURCE

▶ Find another source about the Triangle Shirtwaist Factory fire. Compare the information there to the information in this source.

machine tables, not sure what to do next. They screamed as the fire surrounded them.

I ran to the front elevator, but it was not working. I then joined a group of girls struggling to open a door. We pushed, pulled, and kicked the door. "It's locked!" I screamed over the raging fire.

▲ *Investigators found one of the locked doors of the Triangle Shirtwaist Factory after the fire.*

I spun around and noticed that the door to the back staircase was open. I then said a prayer and wrapped my scarf tightly around my head. The heat was searing. I staggered down the crowded staircase from the ninth floor and passed through the fiery eighth floor. When I reached the bottom floor, a fireman ordered me to stay inside. He said it was unsafe on the street because people were jumping out of the windows to their deaths.

When the fireman let me exit, I spotted Father through my watery eyes. We ran to each other and hugged for a long time. "We've got to find Rosie!" I cried. We searched through the crowd but could not find her.

Later that evening, we visited a temporary **morgue**. Father and I looked at the charred bodies. Some were burned beyond recognition. I stopped abruptly when I noticed one young woman's burned body. On her left hand was a familiar gold ring. I cried hysterically. We had found Rosie.

Mary Robbins

New York Socialite

It has been nearly six months since I graduated from Vassar College in Poughkeepsie, New York. I had such a grand time there! Sadly, those days are gone. I am back at home with my parents and Jane, my 16-year-old sister. We live in a large brownstone on New York City's Upper West Side. We have a **lavish** lifestyle because Father runs a successful iron business.

I was told on more than one occasion that I would never have to work. Even so, boredom set in and I told my parents that I wanted to get a job. "Nonsense, Mary!" Father said. "Your job right now is to find a husband. You're a pretty girl!"

Mother pulled me aside and said that I needed to live a little. Maybe I should join some more clubs, go to parties, or do some volunteer work. I liked the idea of volunteering. It would give me a way to help others. But what could I do?

For weeks, I looked for ways to volunteer. I could not find anything I liked. That all changed on December 15, 1909. A friend of Mother's invited us to a special lunch at the Colony Club. Membership in this women's social club is highly selective. The club offers all kinds of activities. I enjoy the reading room and

THINK ABOUT IT

▶ Determine the main point of this chapter. Pick out one piece of evidence that supports it.

swimming pool. Many club members also help those who are less fortunate.

Approximately 150 members attended the luncheon. Strikers from the garment industry joined us. My eyes teared up when I learned how hard the strikers work to survive. One young Jewish woman spoke of her dying mother and two little sisters she worked to support. She did this all on only $3.50 a week! Another girl who looked even younger than my sister complained about the busy season. During this time, she worked 14-hour days.

Members agreed that the strikers needed help. Two ladies offered their hats for a collection. Within minutes, about $1,300 was collected. The strikers needed this money. It gave them something to live on while they walked the picket lines.

The meeting motivated me to join the Women's Trade Union League (WTUL). It is a group of women from all social classes. Its purpose

is to improve working conditions for women.

Within days, I found myself taking part in a motor parade down Fifth Avenue in the garment district. Graduates from Vassar and other women's colleges joined in. We also helped the garment workers by voicing our support for their strikes. Garment workers were often arrested. The policeman asked why I would want to bother with those uneducated women.

I think we made some progress though. By February 1910, even the most stubborn employers had caved in. Workers at the Triangle Shirtwaist Factory, for example, got shorter working hours. They also got a slight pay raise.

I remained active in the WTUL. Working conditions for women still needed to be improved. Our goal was for all factories to have an eight-hour workday. We also wanted a minimum wage, no night work, and no child labor.

More than a year later, on March 25, 1911, Jane and I were enjoying the spring weather at Washington Square Park. But our peaceful day was shattered. Hopeless screams and blaring sirens sounded up the block. We noticed that the noise came from the Triangle Shirtwaist Factory. Smoke erupted out of the tall structure. We walked toward the building. We were horrified to see people

SECOND SOURCE

▶ Find another source on the garment workers' strike of 1909. Compare the information there to the information in this source.

▲ *Crowds helplessly watched as the fire raged in the Asch Building.*

on the ninth floor standing on window ledges with fire on their backs. Others crowded tightly behind them. Within minutes, the people on the windowsills began jumping off. The nets the firemen used to try to catch them were useless. The bodies just tore through and crashed onto the hard concrete below. Jane and I wept bitterly as we watched the scene before us. I fought hard for the workers at the Triangle. Now many were dead.

On April 5, 1911, Jane and I stood in the pouring rain. We mourned with thousands of others at a funeral procession. It paid tribute to the lives that were lost in the fire. Members of various unions carried banners that said, "We mourn our loss."

Days later, I volunteered for the Joint Relief Committee. Some members of the WTUL and other organizations helped start the committee. My job was to interview survivors of the fire and relatives of the victims. After this, I made suggestions about how we could help the families. This was the least I could do. Something needs to be done. It is my hope that the state of New York improves fire safety in the workplace soon.

DEATH TOLL

The Triangle Shirtwaist Factory fire lasted less than 20 minutes but killed 146 people. Many were recent Jewish and Italian women immigrants. Some women were as young as 14. After the fire, policeman tagged the dead. It took weeks for the bodies to be identified by their loved ones.

Daniel Jones

New York City Firefighter

Firefighting is in my blood. My grandfather, father, and uncle were firemen. I followed in their footsteps. I trained with the New York City Fire Department for Engine Company No. 33. Although I had worked at the company for seven years, it did not prepare me for the Triangle disaster.

The Triangle Shirtwaist
Factory called the fire department
at about 4:45 p.m. on March 25,
1911. I was in the middle of
cleaning one of the horse stalls
when we were dispatched. We have
trained our horses to be ready to
go once we receive a call.

ANALYZE THIS

▶ Analyze two of the accounts of
the Triangle Shirtwaist Factory
Fire in this book. How are they
alike? How are they different?

Within minutes, we arrived in
front of the Asch Building on the corner of
Washington Place and Greene Street. When we got
there, I noticed that many other firehouses answered
the call as well. Flames rose from the eighth floor.
They were pulled into windows on the ninth floor.
Panicked ninth-floor workers stood on window
ledges while flames swirled around them. Many
jumped to their deaths. Our nets could not sustain
their weight. Our horses whinnied and reared on

their hind legs. The screams and loud thuds of bodies hitting the pavement frightened them. I managed to pull the reins tight and keep them in one spot.

Then the crowd started shouting for us to raise the ladders. We tried to raise the ladders, but they only reached the sixth floor.

The captain of our firehouse ordered us to go inside and hose down the eighth floor. Once in the stairwell, the intense fire took us aback. For our own safety, we decided to face the vicious flames by lying on the floor rather than standing. The heat wasn't as intense on the ground. From the floor, we opened the nozzle and blasted the stairway with water.

By 5:15 p.m., we nearly put out the blaze on the eighth, ninth, and tenth floors. There was no reason to celebrate, however. We found charred bodies near windows, by the doors, and in the washrooms. All the workers trapped inside the building were dead.

▲ *Firefighters searched for bodies in a hole through the sidewalk by the Asch Building.*

▲ *Firefighters used their hoses to try to put out the flames in the building.*

When we exited, firefighters began the grim task of finding and lowering the corpses out of the building. I lost count of how many bodies they brought down.

My team arrived back at the firehouse later that night. The whole scene was unsettling. We barely helped those people! Was this all the fire department's fault or was there more to this disaster? Investigators determined that more than one fire escape should have been installed in the building. Even so, the lone fire escape collapsed under the weight of all the people trying to use it. Several of the survivors insisted that they couldn't get out of the building because one of the doors was locked. It is against the law to lock doors during working hours.

THINK ABOUT IT

▶ Determine the main point of this paragraph. Pick out one piece of evidence that supports it.

The district attorney investigated the locked door further. On December 4, the Triangle Shirtwaist Factory owners, Max Blanck and Isaac Harris, were put on trial. They were accused of **manslaughter**. The district attorney tried to prove that the doors were locked. He also tried to show that the locked doors caused many deaths. Several firemen testified at the trial.

Worker after worker said that the door to the Washington Place exit was locked. This was the only usable exit. The door to the Greene Street exit was full of flames. The defense, however, had witnesses who said that there was a key placed in the lock. I wonder who was lying.

I didn't know whom to believe. The judge reminded the jury that there needed to be evidence that the door was locked. They also needed proof that the owners knew the door was locked.

On December 27, the jury found the Triangle owners not guilty. The families cried after the verdict was read.

Investigators believe that someone on the eighth floor carelessly tossed a cigarette butt into a basket of clothing scraps. This caused the scraps to ignite. Although smoking is not allowed in the factories, no one seems to enforce this rule. I hope that some good comes out of the ashes.

NEW FIRE SAFETY LAWS

After the Triangle tragedy, New York City created the Division of Fire Prevention. This led to many workplace fire safety laws. These include fire alarms, fire drills, automatic sprinklers, and limited numbers of people allowed on fire escapes. Laws also banned smoking in factories.

LOOK, LOOK AGAIN

Take a close look at this photograph of the charred remains of a workroom at the Triangle Shirtwaist Factory. Answer the following questions:

1. What would a young woman who worked at the Triangle Shirtwaist Factory think of this picture? How might she feel about the burned workroom?

2. How would a young, wealthy college graduate describe this picture to her friends? What would her friends think when looking at this scene?

3. What would a New York City firefighter tell his family about this scene? How would he feel about how badly the room was damaged?

GLOSSARY

foreman (FOR-muhn) someone who leads a group of workers

immigrant (IM-i-gruhnt) someone who moves to a new country from another

lavish (LAV-ish) costly

manslaughter (MAN-slaw-tur) the crime of killing a person by accident

morgue (MORG) a place where bodies are kept where they can be identified

picket (PIK-it) to stand outside of a place of business to make a protest

strike (STRIKE) to refuse to work because of a difference of opinion with an employer over wages or working conditions

tenement (TEN-uh-muhnt) a poor and crowded apartment building

union (YOON-yuhn) an organized group of workers joined together for a common purpose, such as raising wages

LEARN MORE

Further Reading

Hopkinson, Deborah. *Shutting Out the Sky: Life in the Tenements of New York, 1880–1924.* New York: Orchard Books, 2003.

Landau, Elaine. *The Triangle Shirtwaist Factory Fire.* New York: Children's Press, 2009.

Marrin, Albert. *Flesh and Blood So Cheap: The Triangle Fire and Its Legacy.* New York: Alfred A. Knopf, 2011.

Web Sites

American Experience: Triangle Fire
http://www.pbs.org/wgbh/americanexperience/films/triangle/player/
This site contains general information, biographies, and an online video about the fire.

Remembering the Triangle Factory Fire
http://www.ilr.cornell.edu/trianglefire/
This site from Cornell University contains primary source documents about the fire and the events surrounding it.

The Triangle Fire: 100 Years Later
http://www.laborarts.org/exhibits/thetrianglefire/
This online exhibit is about the garment industry, the Triangle fire, and its aftermath.

INDEX

ABOUT THE AUTHOR

Rachel A. Bailey grew up in a small Kansas town near Kansas City. As a child, she enjoyed reading, bicycling, and taking walks with her beloved Australian shepherd. Rachel is a former teacher. She now writes children's magazine articles and educational curriculum. *The Triangle Shirtwaist Factory Fire* is her third book.